MOODS OF THE
LAKELAND TARNS

J ON S PARKS

HALSGROVE

First published in Great Britain in 2005

British Library Cataloguing-in-Publication Data
A CIP record for this title is available from the British Library

ISBN 1 84114 468 1

HALSGROVE
Halsgrove House
Lower Moor Way
Tiverton, Devon EX16 6SS
Tel: 01884 243242
Fax: 01884 243325
email: sales@halsgrove.com
website: www.halsgrove.com

Printed and bound by D'Auria Industrie Grafiche Spa, Italy

INTRODUCTION

In a very real sense, the Lake District is defined by its lakes, yet the smaller sheets of water, the tarns, are at least as important. For a start, there are far more of them: over 200 have been named, and many others haven't. And they offer much greater variety.

There are tarns large enough to sail on and others too small or shallow even to swim in. They are found at every level, from the valleys to the high fells. And to anyone who likes peace and quiet, who craves solitude or just likes to explore, they offer far wider possibilities than do the lakes.

For some people, there is endless fascination in nit-picking arguments about what is a lake and what is a tarn. There is a fairly broad consensus that there are sixteen or seventeen lakes in the Lake District, though only one (Bassenthwaite) is truly a lake by name – the others are all 'meres' or 'waters'. The most contentious borderline cases are Brothers' Water and Elter Water. Devoke Water is larger than either, and yet is rarely if ever classed as a lake.

Rather than get bogged down in these arguments, I have adopted a simple strategy. I have included all three of these borderline cases – so you can make up your own mind – and beyond that, have used the simplest possible definition of 'tarn': 'any body of water that isn't a lake'.

This gave me the widest possible latitude. It didn't limit me to the named tarns, though I visited as many of them as I could. It also let me include some of the myriad nameless pools that are scattered across the fells. Some of these are larger than some of the named tarns (oops, here we go again...). More to the point, some of them are exquisitely beautiful.

This flexible definition meant that I could decide to investigate an anonymous splodge of blue on the map, with hardly a clue as to what I might find. And it meant that I could also include pools too small or insignificant to feature at all, at least on the 1:25,000 scale maps. There was much happy poring over maps to be done, but a lot more time wandering the fells, which is as good a way to spend time as any that's ever been devised.

In some parts of the district it seems you can hardly move without stumbling across another tarn or pool. The underlying geology and the sculpting action of the glaciers have created areas of marvellously intricate terrain. These are not places that lend themselves to purposeful, straight-line walking; these are places for wandering, waiting to see what's round the next corner.

For anyone who thinks the Lake District is too crowded, my advice is to forsake the popular paths that fixate on the summits. Seek out obscure tarns or nameless blue spots, and you'll get a totally different perspective. At a stroke the Lake District seems bigger, wilder and emptier.

Of course not all the tarns are obscure or nameless or remote. There are many that are well-known: familiar, sociable, comfortable places. There are a few that can be seen without even getting off the bus, and many more that are accessible by very easy walking. For the devotee of solitude, these places are all too easily dismissed, but two things must be said. Firstly, they are popular not just because they are accessible, but because they are beautiful. And secondly, if you go at the right time, you can sometimes have even the most popular, like Tarn Hows, to yourself.

The Lakeland tarns have something to offer just about everyone. And not only is each tarn different from the next, but any given tarn can change its aspect from one day to the next. Sometimes, such is the fickle nature of Lakeland weather, they can change from minute to minute.

With all this variety, a book of 142 photographs can barely scratch the surface. But that's okay with me. I hope this book will inspire you to venture out and gather your own experiences of the tarns. I know I'll be doing so again and again.

Jon Sparks *July 2005*

LAKE DISTRICT NATIONAL PARK

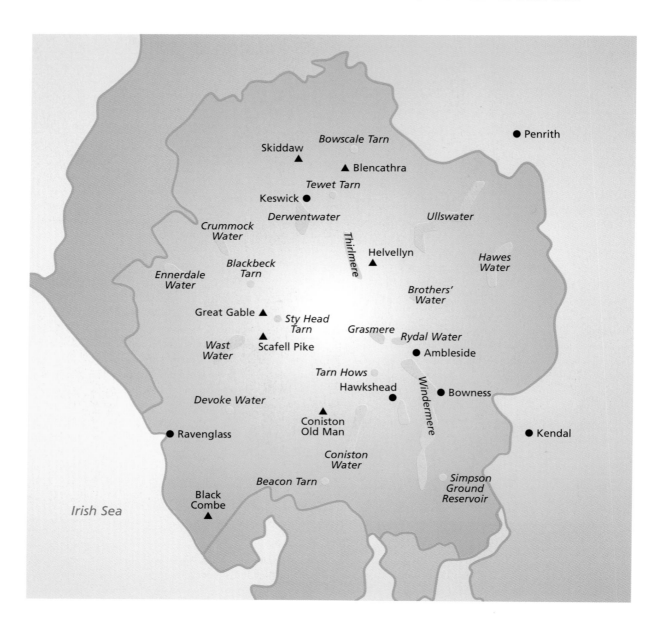

Penrith

Bowscale Tarn

Skiddaw ▲

▲ Blencathra

Tewet Tarn

Keswick ●

Derwentwater

Ullswater

Crummock
Water

Thirlmere

Helvellyn ▲

Hawes
Water

Blackbeck
Tarn

Ennerdale
Water

Brothers'
Water

Great Gable ▲
Sty Head
Tarn

Grasmere

Rydal Water

Wast
Water

Scafell Pike ▲

Ambleside ●

Tarn Hows

Windermere

Hawkshead

Bowness ●

Devoke Water

●

Coniston
Old Man ▲

Ravenglass ●

Kendal ●

Coniston
Water

Beacon Tarn

Simpson
Ground
Reservoir

Black
Combe ▲

Irish Sea

Loughrigg Tarn and the Langdale Pikes
With its perfectly-framed views towards the Langdale Pikes, Loughrigg Tarn
is a gift to photographers and a classic among the lowland tarns.

Bowscale Tarn and Bowscale Fell
There are few tarns in the northern fells – the Skiddaw Slate rocks don't seem conducive to their
formation – but Bowscale Tarn is a textbook example of a glaciated corrie lake. The classic 'armchair'
formation and the deposits of moraine along the lip of the corrie are clearly seen here.

Bowscale Tarn
Too many walkers fixate on summits. The top of Bowscale Fell is relatively unexciting, while its tarn is a far more interesting place, either as the principal objective of a walk or at least somewhere to pause for a while.

Allan Tarn
Allan Tarn is little more than a widening of the River Crake, a little below Coniston Water. However, it has a specific appeal to many visitors as it is the original of the 'Octopus Lagoon' which played a pivotal role in Arthur Ransome's classic children's story, *Swallows and Amazons.*

Beacon Tarn

Beacon Tarn, in the Blawith fells above Coniston Water, also has a special attraction for Arthur Ransome fans, as it's almost certainly the model for Trout Tarn in *Swallowdale*. I crouched low in the shallows of the outlet stream to get this shot.

Low Taggleshaw
A collection of pools rather than a single tarn, Low Taggleshaw lies on Potter Fell, not far from Gurnal Dubs (p22).
It may not be immediately obvious that the water was frozen when this picture was taken,
trapping the bubbles beneath the ice.

Opposite: **High Dam Tarn**
High Dam Tarn, near Newby Bridge, shares many scenic qualities with the much-vaunted Tarn Hows,
but there's a far better chance that you'll have the place to yourself.

Gooseyfoot Tarn

Gooseyfoot Tarn lies deep in Grizedale Forest. The light was low and there was no solid ground to support the tripod for this shot. Thank heavens for digital cameras: I was able to turn up the sensitivity with a twist of a dial. Though I couldn't use a tripod, the camera was level: it's the trees that are leaning!

Opposite: **Reflections, Moss Eccles Tarn**

I like Moss Eccles Tarn a lot, but on this particular afternoon I couldn't find an angle that I was really happy with for a general view. Instead I was drawn by this spindly tree and the enigmatic mix of reflection and transparency.

Anglers, Watendlath Tarn
Watendlath always strikes me as a slightly odd place. There's a faint air of unreality about it, a place to which people come to see the house supposedly inhabited by the fictional heroine, Judith Paris, of a book most of them have never read (the second volume of Hugh Walpole's *The Herries Chronicles*).

Water-lilies, Loughrigg Tarn
Loughrigg Tarn is a popular spot, but rarely gets excessively busy. It's usually possible to find some peace and quiet.

Elter Water, summer evening

Elter Water is one of the borderline cases, frequently classed as a lake rather than a tarn. To me it seems much more tarn-like than Brothers' Water, for example. Anyway, it's too good to miss out and the view towards the Langdale Pikes is a classic.

Willow, Elter Water
The Langdale Pikes were covered in snow, but the willow catkins carried the promise that spring was just around the corner.

Skaters on Tarn Hows

Within living memory it used to be taken for granted that shallower tarns like Tarn Hows would freeze over every winter, and that skating would be possible, often for several weeks at a time. Today, such conditions are exceptional, and when they do occur may only last for a few days.

Opposite: Tarn Hows and Wetherlam

I suppose Tarn Hows is the best-known of all the tarns, the most visited, and the most often photographed. This makes it hard to say anything new about it, but on a perfect winter's day it was still a compelling subject.

Water-lilies on Harrop Tarn
Water-lilies are a familiar sight on many Lakeland tarns in summer. Two species can be
seen in the district: this is the yellow water-lily *Nuphar lutea*.

Opposite: **Water-lily on Dock Tarn**
This is the other species of water-lily which is found: the white water lily *Nymphaea alba*.

Gurnal Dubs

Gurnal Dubs is a distinctively Cumbrian name. 'Dub' is a dialect word meaning 'pool'. It is one of several tarns on Potter Fell, just inside the National Park boundary, north of Kendal. Like many other tarns, its level has been raised by a dam, but its shoreline now looks quite natural.

Detail, Blelham Tarn
Blelham Tarn is a low-lying, reed-fringed tarn just west of Windermere. This pattern of broken
reed-stems appealed at least as much as any of the broader views.

Yew Tree Tarn
With a main road running right by it, Yew Tree Tarn is one of the most widely recognised tarns, but inevitably
not the most peaceful. Still, it's a pretty spot, and the traffic doesn't seem to bother the swans.

Mute Swan, Moss Eccles Tarn
Moss Eccles Tarn was a great favourite with Beatrix Potter, who lived close by in Near Sawrey.
It's said that she kept a little boat on the tarn and would often paddle about, holding
conversations with the ducks and coots. Perhaps the swans were more aloof.

Kentmere Tarn
The original 'mere' of Kentmere was drained in the mid–nineteenth century to create more pasture, and the present tarn is largely formed by flooded workings where the rare diatomaceous earth was excavated. This fossil-rich material has a variety of uses, from insulation to insecticide.

Cuckoo-flower near Burney Tarn
Cuckoo-flower is also known as mayflower or lady's smock.
It's a common plant of damp meadows and wetland margins.

Advancing clouds, Devoke Water
Devoke Water is the largest of the Lakeland tarns and has a fine open situation. Despite this, and despite
being an easy walk from the Birker Fell road, it is relatively little visited.

Clearing clouds, Devoke Water

In the previous shot, the clouds had just rolled over, but the band of light below them gave me confidence that they would clear again, and within half an hour they did just that. The clearance was signalled by the first gleam of light on the water.

Evening, Devoke Water

Perhaps twenty minutes on from the shot on the preceding page, the tarn and its surroundings were bathed in evening sunlight. However, Scafell in the distance remained in cloud. I was really hoping for a spectacular sunset but another mass of cloud lurking in the west put paid to that.

Opposite: **Sow How Tarn**

A pause for contemplation during a hectic mountain-bike ride. The low fells east and south of Windermere have some excellent biking trails, and some lovely tarns too.

Stony Tarn

Stony Tarn doesn't get many visitors; there's only a faint path from nearby Eskdale. I must admit that on a generally cloudy afternoon, I was struggling to find anything compelling to photograph, until I came to the outlet and spotted these ropes of weed in the water. The appearance of a small patch of blue sky was a definite bonus.

Opposite: **Lanty's Tarn**

So who was Lanty? The most famous bearer of the name (a derivative of Lancelot) was Lanty Slee, a notorious distiller and trader in illicit liquor, but it's generally thought unlikely that the tarn was named after him. It remains a mystery to ponder when you visit this little tarn, reached by an easy walk from Patterdale, or better still, Glenridding.

Innominate Tarn and Pillar

Innominate Tarn means the tarn without a name.
It lies on Hay Stacks, a very popular fell between the
Ennerdale and Buttermere valleys. The tarn itself lies
in the middle distance, while the foreground pool
is one of many which also adorn the tangled terrain.
The fell in the background is Pillar.

Opposite: **Pool on Esk Pike**

The long south ridge of Esk Pike gives some of the
grandest and wildest walking anywhere in the Lakes.
On this cold, bright, memorable day I had it entirely
to myself, though I'd seen dozens of people earlier on
Crinkle Crags and Bowfell. Here the background
fells are Scafell and Scafell Pike.

Simpson Ground Reservoir

I had no great expectations of Simpson Ground – a reservoir in the middle of a forestry plantation – so I was pleasantly surprised to find a tarn of very distinctive character, and what might have been a brief visit turned into a lengthy and fascinating exploration.

Lichens by Simpson Ground Reservoir
Lichens are notoriously difficult for the non-specialist to identify conclusively and there's more than one species here: as well as the dominant leaflike ('foliose') one, there is also 'crustose' growth on the seemingly bare rock.
The shot was taken with a macro lens and the whole scene is no more than 10 cm across.

Reflections, Simpson Ground Reservoir
The mirror-like calm of this very sheltered tarn lends itself to shots like this,
which show up the pocketed weathering of the Silurian rocks.

Drowned tree, Simpson Ground Reservoir
Simpson Ground has a number of drowned trees, something I can't recall seeing elsewhere in the district.
Some of the trees are still upright, but I liked this fallen one.

Blackbeck Tarn and Haystacks

When I was photographing at Blackbeck Tarn, I noticed that many walkers passed by with scarcely a second glance, focused on Hay Stacks and Innominate Tarn. Their loss, I thought. Blackbeck Tarn is not only substantially larger than Innominate Tarn, it strikes me it is a more attractive sheet of water.

Opposite: **Detail, by Blackbeck Tarn**

In the process of ranging around a tarn looking for the best angle for a general view, it's common to stumble (sometimes literally) over all sorts of incidental but interesting details.

Pools on Glaramara
Glaramara is a classic example of the tangled scenery of the Borrowdale Volcanic rocks, bristling with crags and peppered with small tarns, most of them nameless. The peak of Bowfell is on the extreme right and Pike o'Blisco is the symmetrical fell left of centre.

Opposite: **Pool on Lang How**
Lang How is a place for wandering, and on a summer's day can be a great place for loitering too, listening to the skylarks and perhaps, at pools like this, looking out for dragonflies.

Damas Dubs and Scafell

Damas Dubs is really the name of the beck that meanders across this high shelf above Eskdale, but as 'dub' means pool, it seems to fit. Pedants may say that the prominent peak is Slight Side, but other pedants will counter that Slight Side is not a separate fell, merely a rise on the south ridge of Scafell. The peaks nearer the centre of the picture are Scafell Pike and Ill Crag.

Detail, Innominate Tarn

I did spend some time trying to get a picture of the many pond-skaters – tiny insects skittering about
on the water surface – but they were too small, too fast and too unpredictable, and in the end
I had to content myself with this static detail.

Boulder near Scoat Tarn

This boulder, close to the outlet of Scoat Tarn, looks as if it has been shattered by some explosion or lightning strike, but it's almost certainly the result of more gradual action by frost.

Opposite: **Sprinkling Tarn and Great End**

Sprinkling Tarn occupies a kind of shelf between Great End and Seathwaite Fell. The popular path between Esk Hause and Sty Head can be seen beyond the tarn, and it's also a favoured spot for camping.

47

Greycrag Tarn
Spot the tarn! This is a 'real' tarn in the sense that it is named as such on OS maps, but there's precious little open water to be seen. Presumably it has silted up and filled in since the name was bestowed. The richness of the wetland vegetation made it a strikingly colourful scene.

Pool in Grizedale Forest
There are many small pools scattered around Grizedale Forest. Some have only come into existence because forestry operations have blocked streams. Others, like this one, are more permanent.

Pool, Little Stand
Little Stand is generally dismissed as merely a shoulder of Crinkle Crags, but for anyone who relishes
a wild walk with grand views and a good chance of being completely alone, it's hard to beat, and it
does have a distinct summit of its own. It's also peppered with small crags and pools.

Opposite: **Walker on Wetherlam**
Wetherlam is one of my favourite fells, partly because on a clear day it's visible from my back garden
in Lancaster, about 25 miles (40 km) away. It is also a complex and interesting hill, with a variety
of routes of ascent including several scrambles. It was after completing one of these that we
came across this little pool. The peak in the background is Swirl How.

Blencathra from Tewet Tarn
Tewet Tarn enjoys a very open situation, giving grand views of surrounding
fells like Helvellyn, Skiddaw and Blencathra.

Opposite: **Cows at Tewet Tarn**
Curious cows can be an infernal nuisance when you're trying to frame a perfect landscape shot. However, while
I liked the view towards Blencathra, I was less happy with the foreground in the view towards
the north-western fells. In the end I decided the cows had done me a favour.

Winter evening, Tarn Hows
Tarn Hows is a much-photographed
subject and when it is busy it can be hard to
concentrate on trying to find a fresh view
of it. But late on a winter afternoon
everything was silent and it was much
easier to appreciate its true beauty.

Pool on Crinkle Crags

In clearer weather I might have paid much less attention to this tiny pool. It is only about three metres to the far shore, which shows just how thick the mist was.

Sty Head Tarn from Seathwaite Fell
Conditions were not promising as I began my descent towards Sty Head Tarn: it wasn't just rain but sleet or soft hail.
At least I could see where I was going, and make out the summits of Great Gable and Green Gable.

Opposite: **Rain at Sty Head Tarn**
Things hadn't improved markedly by the time I reached the shoreline; there was still a wintry quality to the rain.
But Lakeland weather is nothing if not changeable, and there were a few brighter patches in among the clouds.

Angle Tarn

There are two well-known Angle Tarns: this is the one on the north side of Bowfell. On this occasion
the clouds had gathered and it seemed deep in gloom, but a little patience usually brings a reward,
and soon this fleeting glimmer of light appeared.

Opposite: **Sty Head Tarn**

This picture was taken a little over an hour after the one on the previous page. Finally the sun shone
over the tarn and the peaks of Great End, Broad Crag, Scafell Pike and Lingmell.

Stickle Tarn and Pavey Ark
There is another Stickle Tarn, but this is the one everyone is familiar with, above Great Langdale, and one of the
finest tarns in the district. The crags of Pavey Ark appear forbidding, but there's a route up them for
agile walkers known as Jack's Rake, which can be seen rising diagonally from right to left.

Opposite: **Climbing above Stickle Tarn**
Jack's Rake may be the best-known route, but the crags of Pavey Ark have over 70 rock climbs of all levels of difficulty.
The upper reaches of the crags are more than 200 metres above the dark waters of the tarn.

Boulder by Low Water

The geology of the Coniston Fells is particularly complex, and the patchwork appearance of this boulder seems
to symbolise it, though of course much of its colour is actually due to its surface cover of lichens.
But it was its vivid red colour against the green grass that initially caught my eye.

Opposite: **Levers Water**

Levers Water lies above the Coppermines valley in the Coniston Fells. It formerly supplied water to power the mining
operations: the foundations of a large water-wheel still stand in the valley below. A section of the dam can be seen on
the right: otherwise there is little evidence of the industrial past in this view, looking towards Great How Crags.

Blackbeck Tarn
I had secured several shots of Blackbeck Tarn (see p40–41) and was ready to move on. Heading along the shoreline towards the outlet, however, I encountered this jumble of rocks and had to unpack camera and tripod and start again.

Scrambling on Brim Fell

Competent scramblers can ascend to Low Water by way of Low Water Beck, and then continue on above it, almost to the summit ridge of Brim Fell: one of the best ways to the tops of the Coniston Fells.

Rain, Tarn Hows

Pedants will tell you that Tarn Hows should really be called 'The Tarns', and there were indeed several tarns here prior to the construction of a dam in the nineteenth century. However, Tarn Hows is what everyone calls it now. I thought it was appropriate to have a few pictures taken in the rain; without it there would be no tarns or lakes.

Greenburn Tarn and Great Carrs
This is the Greenburn on the northern side of the Coniston Fells (there's another near Grasmere). The sun picks out
the crags of Great Carrs, with the slightly higher peak of Swirl How still in shadow to the left.

Blind Tarn

Blind Tarn, in the Coniston Fells, is so called because there is no surface stream draining from it: obviously the water percolates underground somewhere. It is a fine place for a wild camp, but there's not a lot of flat ground: that's our tent on the best spot.

Opposite: **Kelly Hall Tarn**

I had probably passed along the nearby road a hundred times without ever realising how short a walk it was to Kelly Hall Tarn, or what a great foreground it made for a view of the Coniston Fells. I am sure a lot less time will pass before my next visit.

Stickle Tarn (*also opposite*)

This is the 'other' Stickle Tarn (see p60–61 for its better-known namesake). It lies in the side of Stickle Pike, above the Duddon valley. There was a full gale blowing. Even with the tripod set low, I felt necessary to keep a firm grip on it. But I felt it was worth the trouble as the light was changing almost by the second. Landscape photography isn't always a leisurely, contemplative business: sometimes it demands pretty quick reactions.

Walkers at Innominate Tarn

Innominate Tarn and Hay Stacks are places of pilgrimage for many walkers. The fell was a favourite of the late Alfred Wainwright, author of the famous series of guidebooks, and he requested that his ashes be scattered there.

Rocks near Sprinkling Tarn

I was trying to move fast to get several different views of Sprinkling Tarn during what promised to be a brief sunny spell, but I couldn't resist pausing briefly to record these striking banded rocks.

Seathwaite Tarn
Seathwaite Tarn, on the Duddon side of the Coniston Fells, is one of the largest tarns, though it owes its
present size and shape to a substantial dam, and is still in use as a reservoir.

Opposite: **Pool on Thunacar Knott**
Thunacar Knott is really the parent fell of Pavey Ark, but the latter is a far more coveted objective, leaving
Thunacar Knott relatively peaceful. On the skyline are Crinkle Crags, Bowfell, Scafell Pike and
Great End, with the dark cone of Pike o'Stickle in the middle distance.

Bleaberry Tarn and Chapel Crags
There are advantages in photographing tarns.
I didn't envy the walkers who were just leaving
Bleaberry Tarn as I arrived; they faced a steep
pull up eroded slopes onto Red Pike, while
I roamed around the tarn in the sunshine.

Detail, Bleaberry Tarn
The rocks around Bleaberry Tarn struck me as unusually rich in mosses and lichens.

Low Water
It is a bit of a mystery why Low Water is so called, as it's the highest of the large tarns on the Coniston Fells,
close under the crags of Coniston Old Man and Brim Fell.

Opposite: **Low Water and Coniston Water**
Looking down from high on Brim Fell, Low Water sparkles in sunlight, with Coniston Water beyond. This view also shows the extensive
quarrying nearby on the flanks of Coniston Old Man. The tarn was dammed to provide a water supply for the workings.

Pool on Bell Crags
Bell Crags is one of several significant fells that were, for some reason, not included in the legendary Wainwright guides.
This means you can often have its attractive rocky summit all to yourself. For those who would
like a clue to its location, the fell in the background is Ullscarf.

Cotton-grass, Bell Crags
The fluffy white heads of cotton-grass – also known as bog-cotton – are a common sight around tarns and wetlands in summer.

Detail, Alcock Tarn

I suspect that this is an image that would have been impossible to capture on film: the contrast range
is too extreme. However, with a digital camera, and careful processing of the raw files,
it was possible to bring out nearly all the detail that was visible to the eye.

Opposite: **Alcock Tarn**

Alcock Tarn occupies a shelf on the fells east of Grasmere and like many tarns it has been dammed.
The distant fells include Wetherlam, Swirl How, Crinkle Crags and the Langdale Pikes.

Grisedale Tarn

Grisedale Tarn is at a cross-roads of walkers' routes. The Helvellyn ridge lies to the north and the Fairfield range to the east and south. Between the two, the valley of Grisedale runs down to Ullswater. The notch in the skyline is Grisedale Hause, from where Tongue Gill leads down towards Grasmere; the fell on its right is Seat Sandal.

Opposite: Harrop Tarn and Tarn Crags

Harrop Tarn is on the flanks of Ullscarf, a short walk from the shores of Thirlmere, but seems surprisingly little-visited.

Wise Een Tarn
Wise Een Tarn lies a little higher than Moss Eccles Tarn (p13) on the lovely low ridge
of Claife Heights, a great area for walks or bike rides.

Opposite: **Burnmoor Tarn and Harter Fell**
Burnmoor Tarn is a surprising place, one of the largest of the upland tarns, and the substantial lodge beside it is even more unexpected.
It's easily visited during a fine walk – or mountain-bike ride – between Wasdale and Eskdale.

Foxes Tarn

Foxes Tarn is often stated to be the highest tarn in the district, though this is debatable. It is safe to say that it is the highest tarn with a generally-recognised name. It lies at about 2690ft/820m on the Eskdale side of Scafell. To underline the fickleness of Lakeland weather, this shot was taken little more than an hour after the sunny view of Damas Dubs on p44.

Pool in Lingcove Beck
Lingcove Beck is a tributary of the Esk and
runs down from Bowfell, seen in the distance.
On a hot day this pool looked very tempting,
but the water was icy cold.

Frost on tree, by High Dam Tarn
It was a perfectly still morning, but I knew
that the sun would soon strip the delicate
frost from this little birch sapling.

Opposite: **High Dam Tarn**
High Dam, near Newby Bridge, has many of
the same scenic qualities as the more famous
Tarn Hows, but personally I prefer it. For a
start, there's a much greater chance of having
the place to yourself, as I did on this fine
frosty morning.

Over Water
Over Water is tucked away in the low fells on the northern fringe of the Lake District. Its level has been raised by a lengthy dam/embankment, long since overgrown and colonised by trees, as seen in the foreground.

Trout
There are fish in most of the tarns, of course, but I didn't need an underwater camera to get this image
of a brook trout: it was taken at the Aquarium of the Lakes, near Newby Bridge.

Low Tarn

Low Tarn lies above Wasdale, on the flanks of Red Pike. On the skyline is the Scafell range, with Yewbarrow in the middle distance.

Detail, Bowscale Tarn

Legend has it that the sun never shines on the water of Bowscale Tarn. This photograph clearly disproves that tale, although the tarn does lie in permanent shadow during the depths of winter. The story that stars could be seen reflected in the water at midday is pure fancy, and presumably so is the one that it was home to two immortal fish.

Easedale Tarn
One of the best short walks in the Lake District is from Grasmere, past the waterfalls of Sour Milk Gill, to Easedale Tarn.
You can, of course, continue on to the tops, but it's just as rewarding to spend some time at the tarn.

Opposite: **Pool on Grey Knotts**
There is a cluster of pools on the summit plateau of Grey Knotts, above Borrowdale.
The skyline hills are Bowfell, Esk Pike, Great End and Scafell Pike.

Winter evening, Ludderburn
This area – just south of Birkett Houses Allotment (p139) – boasts no recognised tarns, yet among the mires and blanket bogs there are stretches of open water larger than some of the named tarns.

Slades Beck

I'd gone out with the intention of photographing Carlside Tarn, on the side of Skiddaw, but the clouds descended, and the tarn is a pretty nondescript pool even at the best of times. It seemed like a wasted outing. However, I decided to descend by Slades Beck, which turned out to be a geological cornucopia. There's absolutely nothing exaggerated about this shot: the rock really was that colour.

Ice on Loughrigg Tarn
Like any tarn, Loughrigg changes according to season, weather, and time of day. On this occasion,
there was no wind and no-one else about and the silence was profound.

Icicles, near Small Water
For most of the year these crags are dark and dripping, but they provided
a great demonstration of the way a hard frost can transform things.

Goat's Water and Dow Crag
Dow Crag is one of the finest of Lakeland climbing crags, and a personal favourite of mine. On warm days the rocks can be crowded, but on this chilly May day there were just two pairs of climbers on the cliff.

Goat's Water
I didn't have to do much more than swivel the camera 90 degrees to the left to produce this alternative view of Goat's Water.

Opposite: **Brothers' Water**
Brothers' Water is one of those borderline
cases, sometimes considered to be a lake
rather than a tarn. It is not very big, but
it does occupy the full width of its valley
in a decidedly lake-like manner.

Easedale Tarn
Easedale Beck winds through a maze
of moraines just above the tarn.

Low Water
A small beck enters the tarn here and has obviously washed down this motley collection of pebbles.

Ice on Small Water
The ice was new, still thin and fragile, and it made a pretty good mirror for the surrounding crags.

Dock Tarn

Dock Tarn, above Watendlath, makes a great destination for a short walk, especially on a summer afternoon. 'Dock' is a dialect name for water-lily, so it's no surprise that they grow here in abundance in season.

Opposite: **Wise Een Tarn**

Wise Een Tarn is a place I've been to many times and shall return to many more. This was an afternoon of big clouds and shifting shadows. The highest peak, on the left, is Bowfell, and the familiar shape of the Langdale Pikes is further right.

Jack's Rake and Stickle Tarn
Jack's Rake, an easy scramble in summer, can be a much more serious proposition in winter conditions.

Opposite: **Ice on Sty Head Tarn**
The sun had not quite reached the surface of the tarn, making it all the more effective as a mirror.
An hour later we were climbing, quite comfortably, on the sun-warmed rock of the Napes crags on Great Gable.

Tarn on Seathwaite Fell
This is one of numerous tarns on Seathwaite Fell. Many walkers visit the fell only once, and often briefly,
to tick it off their list of 'Wainwrights', yet it's a complex place that deserves a more leisurely exploration.

Opposite: **Small Water and Haweswater**
The ancient track between Troutbeck and Mardale can be seen climbing up to the left of the tarn in this view from
Nan Bield Pass. The conspicuous white shoreline of Haweswater is due to fluctuating water levels as it is a reservoir.

Red Tarn
Red Tarn is another of those names that occurs more than once. This is the one near Wrynose Pass.
In the background is Great Knott, a shoulder of Crinkle Crags.

Tarn on Holme Fell
The OS map blandly dismisses this as 'Reservoir (disused)'. What could sound less appealing? Yet it's a place
of great charm, even on a misty day, and easily reached from Tilberthwaite.

Round-leaved Crowfoot, by Burney Tarn
Exploring the maze of pools and mires around Burney Tarn (p27),
I found these little white flowers of round-leaved crowfoot.

Opposite: **Above Blea Tarn**
This, of course, is not the Langdale Blea Tarn. This one has a good claim to be the most central tarn in the
Lake District. It lies on the northern slopes of Ullscarf, near the track from Thirlmere to Watendlath.

Scoat Tarn

It is quite a long walk to Scoat Tarn. Having started from Wast Water in bright sunshine, I was feeling frustrated by the way the clouds rolled over before I reached the tarn. But having come that far, I wasn't about to give up straight away. Clambering about above the eastern shore, I came across this remarkable perched boulder, which looked too precarious to even contemplate climbing on to its top.

Scoat Tarn and the Isle of Man
Continuing my explorations, I realised that the Isle of Man was just visible away to the west.

Codale Tarn and Fairfield
Codale Tarn lies above Easedale Tarn and sits on a shelf slightly off to the side from the main path up the valley, so it is often deserted.

Detail, Codale Tarn
I liked the view across to Fairfield, but I was equally taken with the way the heather
had managed to find a foothold on this half-submerged boulder.

Red Tarn and Helvellyn
Red Tarn is one of the classic glaciated tarns of the district, flanked by the sharp arêtes of Striding and Swirral Edges, and backed by steep crags. These are rarely climbed in summer but become popular in good snow conditions.

Summit pool, Seathwaite Fell
Seathwaite Fell has several 'summits' but the knoll just beyond the pool is the highest. The peak beyond is Great Gable.

Mallard drake, High Dam Tarn
Mallard are the commonest duck throughout most of Britain and may be seen on most of the
Lakeland tarns. At High Dam they seemed almost tame and it was very easy to get a
good close-up showing the fine detail in the feathers of this drake.

Opposite: **Long Moss, Torver Back Common**
Long Moss is a good example of a tarn which is gradually silting up and losing its identity.
It lies on Torver Back Common, not far from Kelly Hall Tarn (p68).

125

Burney Tarn
Burney Tarn, on the slopes of the low Woodland Fells, south of Coniston Water, is surrounded by wetland. Without waders, or getting extremely wet and dirty, there was no way I could get close to the edge of the tarn proper.

Reeds, Burney Tarn
Although bright, the day was very windy, and these tall reeds were in constant motion.
I deliberately used a slow shutter speed to try and give an impression of that movement.

Dow Crag and Coniston Old Man from Beacon Tarn
It was a generally cloudy day, with a stiff breeze. A brief parting of the clouds illuminated
the ridge north of the tarn while the fells beyond were in deep shadow.

Opposite: **Walkers on Long Top, Crinkle Crags**
This pool on Long Top, near the summit of Crinkle Crags, is larger than Foxes' Tarn (p88) and at much the
same height, yet has no name. Lying off to one side from the main ridge, it is missed by many walkers.
In fact I'm beginning to have second thoughts: maybe I should have kept it a secret.

Settlement, Woodland Fell
The pursuit of tarns has led me to a number of discoveries. I'd seen from the map that Woodland Fell had a several ancient sites, but it was the presence of a collection of pools that finally led me to explore the area in more detail. I hadn't expected the settlement to be so extensive or so clear on the ground. On closer investigation, the whole area is liberally sprinkled with cairns, hut circles and other prehistoric remains.

Tarn on Woodland Fell

It was this tarn that had originally drawn me to the vicinity, but once I found the ancient remains, photographing the tarn became little more than an afterthought. The fell seen in the distance is Black Combe.

Scales Tarn and Sharp Edge

There are only two significant tarns in the northern fells – Bowscale Tarn (p6–7) and Scales Tarn – but they are both very fine. Scales Tarn shares with Bowscale Tarn the legend that the sun never reaches its surface. Sharp Edge, which forms the skyline, is a classic glacial arête and second only to Striding Edge in the pecking order of walkers' scrambles.

Mire below Coniston Old Man

This extensive mire is a stone's throw from the spot where many walkers leave their cars at the start of the Walna Scar track, which can be seen just beyond. It's not named or marked on the OS Explorer map, yet a little further along the track, Boo Tarn is still indicated, though there's now little more to it than a patch of rushes.

Eel Tarn

Eel Tarn lies on a broad upland above the middle reaches of Eskdale. It is usually quiet, though a pair of greylag geese made a brief but extremely noisy visit while I was there. The peak in cloud is Kirk Fell.

Opposite: **Lily Tarn**

It is a shade ironic that there are no lilies in evidence in this winter view: in summer the name is well-merited. The tarn lies on a shoulder of Loughrigg Fell, close to Ambleside. The peaks of Froswick, Ill Bell and Wansfell Pike punctuate the skyline.

135

Yew Tree Tarn
This shot takes almost exactly the reverse angle of the one on p24.

Opposite: **Pool on Lang How**
Lang How sports a number of pools (see also p43), of which this is the largest. Beyond is the head
of Great Langdale, hemmed in by Pike o'Blisco, Crinkle Crags, Bowfell and the Langdale Pikes.

Miterdale, Burnmoor Tarn and Scafell

Burnmoor Tarn lies below Scafell and at the head of Miterdale. The little valley within a valley, seen here at bottom right, has been suggested as the original of Arthur Ransome's 'Swallowdale'. This is probably not the case – Ransome's stamping grounds were around Windermere and Coniston – but it does have the right kind of secret atmosphere.

Tarn on Birkett Houses Allotment

Birkett Houses Allotment is just east of the southern reaches of Windermere and just north of Ludderburn (see p98). Despite very easy access from busy Bowness, it attracts surprisingly few visitors, probably because it has no named tarns or summits.

Sprinkling Tarn, Esk Pike and Great End
I make no apologies for including a second shot of lovely Sprinkling Tarn. This view shows
its distinctive shape: in fact it is very nearly two separate tarns.

Opposite: **Easedale Tarn**
Easedale Tarn is a deservedly popular spot, but there was a stillness about it on this chilly morning.
This view is from close to the outlet of the tarn, looking up towards Blea Rigg.

Angle Tarn
This is the Angle Tarn in the far eastern fells, above Patterdale. Fairfield is left of centre and St Sunday Crag
to the right, separated by the notch of Deepdale Hause. Helvellyn is on the far right.